Elizabeth M. Potter /
Beatrix Potter

Beatrix Potter
Painting Book part 5

AF176102

by
Elizabeth M. Potter

Content	Page

Bibliografische Information der Deutschen Nationalbibliothek:
Die Deutsche Nationalbibliothek verzeichnet diese Publikation in der Deutschen
Nationalbibliografie; detaillierte bibliografische
Daten sind im Internet über http://dnb.dnb.de abrufbar.

Herstellung und Verlag: BoD – Books on Demand, Norderstedt

ISBN: 9783752866414